Things That Float and Things That Don't

by David A. Adler

illustrated by Anna Raff

Holiday House / New York

With love to my great-nephew, Pinchas Eliyahu
—D. A. A.

For my big brother, Ed
—A. S. R.

Text copyright © 2013 by David A. Adler
Illustrations copyright © 2013 by Anna Raff
All Rights Reserved
HOLIDAY HOUSE is registered in the U.S. Patent and Trademark Office.
Printed and Bound in July 2015 at Toppan Leefung, DongGuan City, China.
The artwork was created with sumi ink washes and drawings,
and assembled digitally.
www.holidayhouse.com
5 7 9 10 8 6 4

Library of Congress Cataloging-in-Publication Data
Adler, David A.
Things that float and things that don't /
by David A. Adler ; illustrated by Anna Raff. — First edition.
pages cm
ISBN 978-0-8234-2862-5 (hardcover)
1. Floating bodies—Juvenile literature. 2. Hydrostatics—Juvenile literature.
3. Buoyant ascent (Hydrodynamics)—Juvenile literature.
I. Raff, Anna, illustrator. II. Title.
QC147.5.A35 2013
532'.25—dc23
2012045827

ISBN 978-0-8234-3176-2 (paperback)

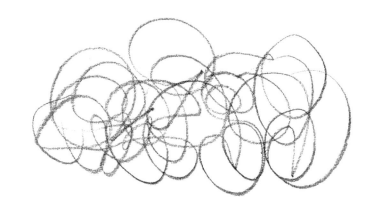

Our world is covered with rivers, lakes, seas, and oceans. More than two-thirds of the surface of the earth is covered with water.

Before there were planes, people traveled across oceans from one continent to the next. They traveled and moved things over rivers and across lakes. Of course, before they could travel or move things by water, they had to know what things float and what things don't.

A large boat that might weigh thousands of pounds will float.

A whole crowd of people could be on that boat, and it would still float. But if one of those people dropped a small pebble into the water, that pebble would sink quickly. Pebbles don't float.

You could have fun guessing which things float and which things don't.

Fill your sink about halfway with water. Get a penny. A penny doesn't weigh much; but if you put it on the surface of the water, it falls right to the bottom. It doesn't float.

Get an empty plastic soda bottle. Fill it about halfway with water. It's much heavier than a penny, but see what happens when you put it in the sink. It floats.

Find things around the house, things that won't be damaged by water. Make a list of what you found. Next to each item on the list write whether you think it will float.

One by one, put each item in the sink.

How often did you predict correctly which things float and which things don't?

It's not just weight that determines whether something will float. It's also the object's size and shape.

Does it float?

	my guess	the answer
pail	yes	yes
apple	yes	yes
marble	yes	no
car	no	no

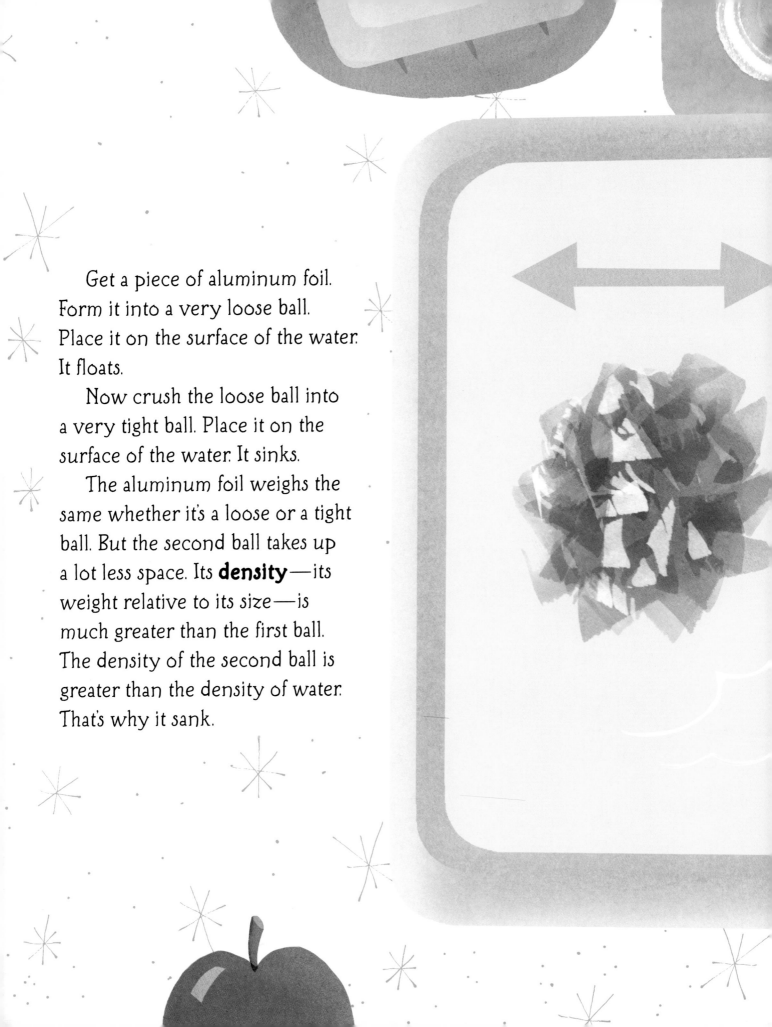

Get a piece of aluminum foil. Form it into a very loose ball. Place it on the surface of the water. It floats.

Now crush the loose ball into a very tight ball. Place it on the surface of the water. It sinks.

The aluminum foil weighs the same whether it's a loose or a tight ball. But the second ball takes up a lot less space. Its **density**—its weight relative to its size—is much greater than the first ball. The density of the second ball is greater than the density of water. That's why it sank.

What's the density of water?

Have you ever filled a bucket with water and tried to lift it? Water is heavy. A **cubic foot** of water—enough water to fill a box one foot high, one foot wide, and one foot deep—weighs a bit more than sixty-two pounds.

That's a lot!

Something has a lower density than water if it weighs less than sixty-two pounds per cubic foot.

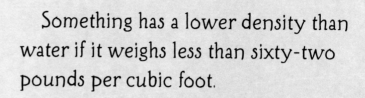

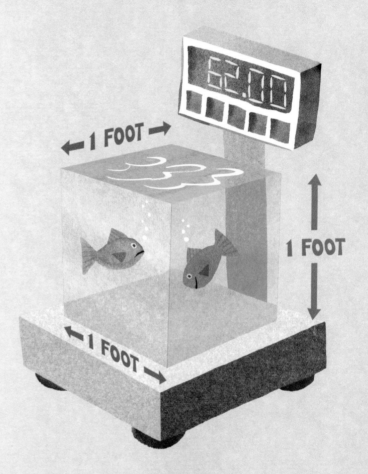

← 1 FOOT →

1 FOOT

← 1 FOOT →

Something with a lower density than water will float.

Do apples float?
One cubic foot of apples weighs about forty pounds. That's less than the density of water. Apples float.

Does a bar of soap float?
One cubic foot of soap weighs about fifty pounds. That's less than the density of water. Soap floats.

40lbs.

50lbs.

Does clay float?

One cubic foot of clay weighs about one hundred pounds. The density of clay is much greater than the density than water. A lump of clay does not float.

But clay **can** float.

Get some modeling clay. Place
a lump of clay on the surface of
the water in your bath.
It sinks.

Now let's make it float.
Shape the clay into a boat. Place the boat on the
surface of the water. Does it sink or float?
The lump of clay and the boat made from it weigh
the same. But the boat takes up more space than the
lump of clay. Because of its shape, the boat encloses
air. The density of the boat and the air it encloses is
less than the density of the water. That's why it floats.

Now, with the clay boat in the water, take a look at the sides of the boat. The boat is not really floating on the water. It's floating *in* the water. Part of it is beneath the surface.

Put a few coins, marbles, or pebbles in the boat.

As the boat and its contents get heavier, more of the boat goes beneath the surface. As the clay boat sinks lower, it pushes water aside. It **displaces** water. The weight of the water the clay boat displaces equals the weight of the boat and its contents.

Because of the shape of a boat, part of its contents is air.

The boat will continue to float if the density of the boat and its contents is less than the density of the water.

Steel is about eight times as dense as water. A cube of solid steel would quickly sink. But the hulls of large boats are made of steel. Boats made of steel float because of their shape.

Now get some ice cubes. Drop the ice cubes in the sink. They float! Why does ice float?

Ice is water.

Icebergs are huge floating mountains of ice found in the colder parts of the world's oceans.

Why do ice and icebergs float?
You can find the answer in your freezer.

Put some water in a paper cup. Make a mark on the side of the cup to show the level of the water. Put the cup in the freezer and wait until the water has completely turned to ice.

The level of the ice is higher than the mark you made on the side of the cup. When water freezes, it expands. Ice weighs the same as water, but ice takes up more space. The density of ice is slightly less than the density of water. That's why it floats.

Not all water is the same.

Have you ever been to a beach? Was the beach at the edge of an ocean or was it on a lake?

Ocean water and lake water are different. Ocean water is salty. Lake water isn't.

Ocean water is denser than lake water. Some things will float in an ocean but sink in a lake.

You can prove that the density of salt water is greater than the density of plain water.

Get an empty plastic soda bottle with a cap. Fill the bottle about halfway with water. Mark the side of the bottle to show how much water is in the bottle. Now add about a teaspoon of table salt to the water. Put the cap on the bottle and shake.

If you check the level of the water, you'll probably *see* that it did not change.
What happened to the salt?

It **dissolved**.

What was once plain water is now salt water. It takes up the same space, but there's more to it. If you checked, you'd find that it weighs more. The density of salt water is greater than the density of plain water. Of course, the saltier the water, the greater its density.

Different things have different densities. Even different kinds of water have different densities. That's why some things float and some things don't.